Real Estate Riches

Strategies for Building Wealth Through Property Investment

Riley Anderson

Copyright © 2024 Riley Anderson

All rights reserved.

DEDICATION

To all those who strive for fulfillment in their careers,

This book is dedicated to you.

May its pages offer guidance, inspiration, and support

as you navigate the twists and turns of your professional journey.

Your dedication to finding meaning and satisfaction in your work

inspires us all to reach for our highest aspirations.

May you find fulfillment, purpose, and joy

in every step you take towards your dreams.

This is for you.

CONTENTS

- ACKNOWLEDGMENTS 1
- **CHAPTER 1** 1
- Building Your Foundation 1
  - 1.1 Why Real Estate? Exploring the Advantages and Risks 1
  - 1.2 Know Yourself: Defining Your Investment Goals and Risk Tolerance 4
  - 1.3 Financial Fitness: Building a Solid Foundation for Investment ... 5
  - 1.4 Education is Key: Resources for Real Estate Knowledge Acquisition 7
- **CHAPTER 2** 10
- Unveiling the Investment Landscape 10
  - 2.1 Residential vs. Commercial Real Estate: Choosing Your Path ... 10
  - 2.2 Understanding Property Types: Single-Family Homes, Multi-Units, and More 13
  - 2.3 Location, Location, Location: Market Analysis and Property Selection 16
  - 2.4 Numbers Don't Lie: Financial Analysis and Due Diligence 19
- **CHAPTER 3** 23
- Stepping on the Property Ladder: Strategies for Novice Investors 23
  - 3.1 The Power of Buy-and-Hold: Building Long-Term Wealth 23
  - 3.2 House Hacking: Living Large While Building Equity 25
  - 3.3 Consider REITs: Investing in Real Estate Without Direct Ownership 27
  - 3.4 Crowdfunding: A Modern Approach to Real Estate Investment .. 29
- **CHAPTER 4** 33
- Mastering the Buy-and-Hold Strategy 33
  - 4.1 Tenant Selection: Finding Reliable Occupants for Your Property. 33
  - 4.2 Property Management: Delegation or DIY? 35
  - 4.3 Maintenance and Repairs: Budgeting and Upkeep Strategies . 38
  - 4.4 Tax Advantages: Leveraging Tax Benefits of Real Estate Ownership 40

CHAPTER 5 44

Rehabilitation and Resale: The Fix-and-Flip Approach............................ 44

    5.1 Identifying Fixer-Upper Opportunities: Spotting Diamonds in the Rough.. 44

    5.2 Renovation Planning and Budgeting: Prioritizing Projects and Costs... 46

    5.3 The Art of the Flip: Marketing and Selling Your Renovated Property.. 48

    5.4 Exiting Strategies: Maximizing Profit When Selling Your Investment... 50

    5.5 Beyond the Basics: Advanced Fix-and-Flip Strategies.............. 52

CHAPTER 6 55

Advanced Strategies for Experienced Investors.. 55

    6.1 BRRRR Method: Renovation, Rental, Refinance, Repeat......... 55

    6.2 Real Estate Investment Groups (REIGs): Pooling Resources for Bigger Deals.. 58

    6.3 Private Lending: Becoming the Bank for Real Estate Investors 61

    6.4 Commercial Real Estate: Higher Risks, Potentially Higher Rewards.. 64

CHAPTER 7 68

Financing Your Real Estate Investments.. 68

    7.1 Traditional Mortgage Options: Understanding Loan Types and Qualifications... 68

    7.2 Hard Money Lenders: Alternative Financing for Quick Deals.. 71

    7.3 House Hacking Mortgages: Financing Strategies for Owner-Occupied Investments... 73

    7.4 Creative Financing Techniques: Seller Financing and Lease Options... 76

CHAPTER 8 79

Legal Considerations and Asset Protection... 79

    8.1 Entity Formation: Choosing the Right Structure for Your Investments.. 79

    8.2 Landlord-Tenant Laws: Understanding Your Rights and Responsibilities.. 82

    8.3 Real Estate Contracts: Navigating the Legal Landscape with

Confidence..84

8.4 Insurance Strategies: Protecting Your Investments from Unexpected Events... 86

CHAPTER 9... **90**

Weathering the Storm: Managing Risk in Real Estate...............................90

9.1 Market Fluctuations: Strategies for Volatile Economic Conditions..90

9.2 Vacancy Rates and Tenant Turnover: Minimizing Rental Income Disruptions...92

9.3 Property Damage and Maintenance Issues: Building Reserves and Risk Mitigation... 94

9.4 Legal Challenges: Addressing Lawsuits and Disputes.............96

CHAPTER 10..**100**

The Long Game: Building a Sustainable Real Estate Portfolio...................100

10.1 Diversification Strategies: Spreading Your Investments Across Markets and Property Types.. 100

10.2 Goal Setting and Portfolio Rebalancing: Keeping Your Investments Aligned with Objectives..103

10.3 Building a Team of Experts: Realtors, Property Managers, and Financial Advisors.. 105

10.4 The Future of Real Estate: Emerging Trends and Technological Advancements.. 107

ABOUT THE AUTHOR... **111**

ACKNOWLEDGMENTS

I would like to express my heartfelt gratitude to everyone who contributed to the creation of this book.

First and foremost, I am deeply thankful to my family for their unwavering support, patience, and encouragement throughout this journey. Your belief in me has been a constant source of strength.

I extend my sincere appreciation to my friends and colleagues who provided valuable insights, feedback, and encouragement along the way. Your perspectives enriched this project in ways I could never have imagined.

I am grateful to the mentors and educators who have guided and inspired me with their wisdom and expertise. Your mentorship has been instrumental in shaping my understanding of career fulfillment.

A special thank you to the readers who have embraced this book. Your curiosity and eagerness to learn motivate me to continue sharing knowledge and insights.

Lastly, I want to acknowledge the countless individuals who have shared their stories, experiences, and expertise in the field of career development. Your collective wisdom has laid the foundation for this work, and I am deeply grateful for your contributions.

Thank you all for being part of this journey.

CHAPTER 1

Building Your Foundation

Welcome to the exciting world of real estate investing! This journey, like any successful endeavor, requires a strong foundation. This chapter will equip you with the essential knowledge and self-awareness to embark on your path to becoming a real estate pro.

1.1 Why Real Estate? Exploring the Advantages and Risks

Real estate has long been a cornerstone of wealth creation. Here's why it continues to be a compelling investment option:

- **Tangible Asset:** Unlike stocks or bonds, real estate is a physical property you can see and touch. This tangibility can provide a sense of security and control over your investment.

- **Steady Income:** Owning rental properties offers the potential for consistent cash flow through rent payments. This income stream can supplement your main income or even replace it entirely when your portfolio grows.

- **Appreciation Potential:** Over time, property values tend to appreciate, meaning your investment can grow in value alongside the market. This trend provides the potential for significant returns when you sell.

- **Tax Advantages:** Real estate ownership offers various tax benefits, including deductions for depreciation, mortgage interest, and property taxes. These deductions can significantly reduce your taxable income.

- **Hedge Against Inflation:** Real estate historically performs well during inflationary periods. As the cost of living increases, so does the rental income you can command, offering a natural hedge against inflation.

However, real estate investment also comes with inherent risks:

- **Market Fluctuations:** The real estate market can be cyclical, with periods of boom and bust. Your property value could decline during a downturn, impacting your potential returns.
- **Vacancy Rates:** Periods where your property sits unoccupied can disrupt your cash flow. Understanding vacancy rates and tenant turnover in your target market is crucial.
- **Management Responsibilities:** Being a landlord requires property management skills, including tenant screening, maintenance coordination, and potentially dealing with repairs and evictions.
- **Illiquidity:** Unlike stocks that can be easily bought and sold, real estate is a less liquid asset. Selling a property can take time and involve additional costs.
- **Significant Upfront Investment:** Down payments

and closing costs can be a significant hurdle for new investors. Carefully evaluating your financial resources is essential.

Understanding these advantages and risks allows you to make informed decisions and choose a real estate investment strategy that aligns with your goals and risk tolerance.

1.2 Know Yourself: Defining Your Investment Goals and Risk Tolerance

Before diving headfirst into the market, take a step back and consider your motivations. Here are some questions to get you started:

- **What are your long-term financial goals?** Are you looking for steady income, capital appreciation, or a combination of both?
- **What is your risk tolerance?** Are you comfortable with the potential for market fluctuations and

property value declines?

- **How much time can you dedicate to managing your investments?** Are you comfortable with the hands-on aspects of being a landlord, or would you prefer a more passive approach?
- **What is your investment timeline?** Are you looking for short-term returns (flipping properties) or long-term wealth creation through buy-and-hold strategies?

By clearly defining your goals and risk tolerance, you can choose an investment strategy that fits your personality and financial circumstances.

1.3 Financial Fitness: Building a Solid Foundation for Investment

Just like building a house requires a strong foundation, so too does real estate investment. Here are some key financial considerations:

- **Down Payment:** Most traditional mortgages require a down payment, typically ranging from 15% to 20% of the property's purchase price. Having a larger down payment reduces your loan amount and monthly mortgage payment.

- **Emergency Fund:** Unexpected repairs, vacancies, or market downturns can disrupt your cash flow. Having a healthy emergency fund provides a safety net and allows you to weather temporary challenges.

- **Credit Score:** A good credit score qualifies you for better interest rates on mortgages, reducing your borrowing costs and maximizing your return on investment.

- **Debt Management:** High-interest debt can hinder your ability to save for a down payment or qualify for favorable loans. Managing existing debt is crucial for a successful real estate investment journey.

- **Investment Capital:** Beyond the down payment and closing costs, consider ongoing expenses like maintenance, property taxes, and potential vacancies. Ensure you have sufficient capital to cover these costs.

By establishing a healthy financial foundation, you'll be better positioned to seize investment opportunities and navigate any challenges that arise.

1.4 Education is Key: Resources for Real Estate Knowledge Acquisition

- **Books and eBooks:** Numerous books and eBooks cover various real estate investment topics, from beginner guides to advanced strategies. Look for publications with good reviews and recommendations from successful investors.
- **Real Estate Investment Websites and Blogs:** Several websites and blogs offer valuable information and insights into the real estate market, investment strategies, and current trends. Choose reputable sources with well-researched content.

- **Real Estate Investment Seminars and Workshops:** Attending seminars or workshops can provide an immersive learning experience. These events offer opportunities to network with other investors and learn from experienced professionals.
- **Real Estate Investment Podcasts:** Podcasts offer a convenient way to learn while you commute, exercise, or do chores. Many podcasts are hosted by successful investors and cover a wide range of real estate topics.
- **Government and Industry Resources:** Government agencies and industry associations often provide valuable resources, including market data, investment guides, and educational materials.
- **Mentorship:** Finding a mentor with real estate experience can be invaluable. A mentor can offer guidance, answer your questions, and provide real-world insights into the investment process.

Additional Tips:

- **Develop a Real Estate Network:** Surround yourself with successful real estate investors, realtors, property managers, and other professionals in the industry. Learning from their experiences and building connections can open doors to new opportunities.

- **Stay Up-to-Date on Market Trends:** Real estate markets are constantly evolving. By staying informed about economic conditions, local market trends, and potential regulatory changes, you can make more informed investment decisions.

By actively seeking knowledge and building a strong foundation, you'll be well-equipped to navigate the exciting and potentially lucrative world of real estate investing. Remember, success doesn't happen overnight, so be patient, stay committed to learning, and enjoy the journey!

CHAPTER 2

Unveiling the Investment Landscape

Congratulations! You've established a strong foundation for your real estate investment journey. Now, it's time to delve into the diverse landscape of investment opportunities.

2.1 Residential vs. Commercial Real Estate: Choosing Your Path

The real estate world offers two primary avenues for investors: residential and commercial. Understanding the key differences between these two sectors will help you choose the path best suited to your goals and risk tolerance.

Residential Real Estate:

- **Property Types:** Single-family homes, multi-unit buildings (duplexes, triplexes, apartment buildings), condominiums, and townhouses.

- **Investment Strategies:** Buy-and-hold for rental income and potential appreciation, fix-and-flip for short-term profits, and house hacking (living in a multi-unit property while renting out other units).
- **Pros:** Typically lower entry point compared to commercial properties, readily available financing options, familiar market dynamics for many investors.
- **Cons:** Potentially higher management responsibilities (dealing with tenants, repairs), lower economies of scale compared to larger commercial properties, greater vulnerability to market fluctuations impacting smaller properties.

Commercial Real Estate:

- **Property Types:** Office buildings, retail spaces, industrial warehouses, hotels, and self-storage facilities.
- **Investment Strategies:** Typically buy-and-hold for

rental income, often requiring active property management or partnerships with experienced commercial operators.

- **Pros:** Potentially higher and more stable rental income compared to residential properties, economies of scale with larger buildings, diversification benefits across different commercial sectors.

- **Cons:** Higher entry cost and often complex financing requirements, greater reliance on professional management expertise, longer lease terms with tenants, susceptibility to economic downturns impacting specific industries (e.g., office vacancy rates during recessions).

Factors to Consider When Choosing Your Path:

- **Investment Goals:** Are you prioritizing steady cash flow, capital appreciation, or a combination of both?

- **Risk Tolerance:** Are you comfortable with the potentially higher volatility and management complexities of commercial properties?

- **Available Capital:** Commercial properties can have a significantly higher entry point compared to residential options.

- **Time Commitment:** Commercial properties often require more active management or reliance on professional services.

By carefully considering these factors, you can choose the real estate path that best aligns with your goals, risk tolerance, and financial resources.

2.2 Understanding Property Types: Single-Family Homes, Multi-Units, and More

Once you've chosen your residential or commercial path, it's time to explore the various property types within that category. Each type offers unique advantages and drawbacks, and understanding these nuances will help you select the investment that best suits your strategies.

Residential Property Types:

- **Single-Family Homes:** Often the most familiar option, offering potential for long-term appreciation and manageable management responsibilities. Ideal for buy-and-hold strategies or starter investors.

- **Multi-Unit Buildings:** Provide the opportunity for higher rental income and economies of scale compared to single-family homes. However, they also come with increased management complexities and potential tenant turnover challenges.

- **Condominiums and Townhouses:** Offer a good balance between single-family home ownership and multi-unit investment. Shared amenities and maintenance responsibilities can reduce some management burden.

Commercial Property Types:

- **Office Buildings:** Provide steady rental income from businesses, but vacancy rates can be a concern, particularly during economic downturns.

- **Retail Spaces:** Offer high foot traffic and potentially strong rental income, but success depends heavily on location and tenant type.
- **Industrial Warehouses:** In high demand due to e-commerce growth, offering stable income but requiring specific tenant needs and potentially large upfront costs.
- **Hotels and Self-Storage Facilities:** Specialized sectors with unique considerations, often requiring significant capital investment and industry expertise.

Researching Property Types:

- **Market Trends:** Analyze current and projected demand for different property types within your target market.
- **Rental Rates and Vacancy Rates:** Understand the potential rental income and likelihood of tenant turnover for a specific type of property.
- **Management Requirements:** Assess the level of

management involvement needed for different property types.

- **Maintenance Costs:** Consider the typical maintenance costs associated with various property types.

By thoroughly researching different property types, you'll be well-equipped to identify investment opportunities that fit your skillset and strategic goals.

2.3 Location, Location, Location: Market Analysis and Property Selection

The old adage in real estate remains true: "Location, location, location." Choosing the right market and property location is crucial for your investment's success. Here's what you need to consider:

- **Market Analysis:**

    - **Economic Conditions:** A strong local

economy with job growth translates to higher rental demand and potentially increasing property values.

- **Population Demographics:** Understanding the demographics of the target area (age, income levels, renter vs. owner ratio) helps identify suitable property types and tenant profiles.
- **Real Estate Market Trends:** Analyze recent sales data, rental rates, and vacancy rates to understand market conditions and potential future trends.
- **Development and Infrastructure:** Planned infrastructure projects or new developments in an area can positively impact property values.
- **Crime Rates and Safety:** A safe neighborhood with low crime rates attracts tenants and can positively impact property value.

- **Property Location:**

  - **Accessibility:** Consider proximity to transportation, schools, job centers, and amenities.
  - **Curb Appeal and Neighborhood Conditions:** A well-maintained property in a desirable neighborhood attracts better tenants and commands higher rent.
  - **Zoning Regulations:** Ensure the property zoning allows for your intended use (residential, commercial, etc.).
  - **Potential for Appreciation:** Look for areas with historical appreciation trends or potential for future development.

Market Research Tools:

- **Local MLS (Multiple Listing Service):** Provides data on recent sales, property details, and market trends.

- **Real Estate Market Reports:** Offered by industry organizations or brokerages, these reports provide valuable insights into local market conditions.

- **Government Websites:** Local government websites often offer data on demographics, development plans, and zoning regulations.

- **Online Mapping Tools:** Tools like Google Maps can help visualize property locations, amenities, and neighborhood demographics.

2.4 Numbers Don't Lie: Financial Analysis and Due Diligence

Before committing to any property, a thorough financial analysis is essential. This process involves crunching numbers and uncovering potential issues to ensure the investment aligns with your financial goals.

Financial Analysis:

- **Purchase Price:** Consider the asking price, potential negotiation room, and closing costs.
- **Rental Income:** Research average rental rates for similar properties in the chosen location.
- **Operating Expenses:** Factor in ongoing costs like property taxes, insurance, maintenance, and property management fees.
- **Capital Expenditures:** Budget for potential repairs, renovations, or replacements that may be needed.
- **Return on Investment (ROI):** Calculate the projected cash flow, potential for appreciation, and overall return on investment based on your projections.

Due Diligence:

- **Property Inspection:** Hire a qualified inspector to identify any structural issues, code violations, or potential repair needs.

- **Title Search:** Ensure the seller has clear ownership of the property and there are no outstanding liens or claims.

- **Review Leases (if applicable):** If the property has existing tenants, understand the terms of their leases and any potential challenges.

- **Review Property History:** Research the property's history to uncover any past issues or environmental concerns.

By conducting a thorough financial analysis and due diligence process, you'll be able to make informed decisions and avoid costly surprises down the road. Remember, real estate is a significant investment, so take your time, gather all the necessary information, and don't hesitate to seek professional advice from experienced real estate agents, financial advisors, or property management companies.

By mastering the art of market analysis, property selection, and financial due diligence, you'll be well on your way to unlocking lucrative opportunities in the ever-evolving real estate landscape.

CHAPTER 3

Stepping on the Property Ladder: Strategies for Novice Investors

Welcome, aspiring real estate mogul! Here, we'll explore entry points that can help you build a solid foundation and take your first steps towards long-term wealth creation.

3.1 The Power of Buy-and-Hold: Building Long-Term Wealth

The buy-and-hold strategy represents the cornerstone of real estate investment. Here's how it works:

- **The Core Idea:** You purchase a property, rent it out to tenants, and generate consistent rental income over time. Additionally, you benefit from potential appreciation in the property value over the long term.

Benefits of Buy-and-Hold:

- **Steady Cash Flow:** Rental income provides a predictable and reliable stream of income, offering financial security and potentially supplementing your primary income.
- **Long-Term Appreciation:** Historically, real estate values tend to increase over time, allowing you to accumulate wealth through property value growth.
- **Tax Advantages:** Real estate ownership offers various tax benefits, including deductions for depreciation, mortgage interest, and property taxes. These deductions can significantly reduce your taxable income.
- **Hedge Against Inflation:** Rising inflation often leads to increased rental income, allowing your investment to keep pace with the rising cost of living.

Considerations for Buy-and-Hold Investors:

- **Down Payment and Closing Costs:** These upfront expenses can be a significant hurdle for new investors.

- **Management Responsibilities:** Being a landlord requires tenant screening, maintenance coordination, and potentially dealing with repairs and evictions. Consider hiring a property management company if you prefer a more passive approach.

- **Market Fluctuations:** The real estate market can experience downturns, impacting property values and potentially leading to temporary vacancy periods.

3.2 House Hacking: Living Large While Building Equity

House hacking offers a creative way for beginners to enter the real estate market with a lower initial investment. Here's the concept:

- **The Strategy:** You purchase a multi-unit property

(duplex, triplex, etc.) and live in one unit while renting out the remaining units. The rental income helps offset your mortgage payment, and you gradually build equity in the property.

Benefits of House Hacking:

- **Lower Barrier to Entry:** By living in one unit, you significantly reduce your housing expenses, freeing up more capital for a down payment.
- **Equity Building:** As you make mortgage payments, you build equity in the entire property, not just the unit you occupy.
- **Learning by Doing:** House hacking provides hands-on experience with property management, tenant relations, and real estate ownership.

Considerations for House Hackers:

- **Financing Options:** Not all traditional mortgages allow owner-occupied multi-unit properties. Explore FHA loans or specialized financing options for house hacking.

- **Lifestyle Considerations:** Living in close proximity to tenants may not be ideal for everyone. Be prepared for potential maintenance issues that disrupt your living space.

- **Local Regulations:** Some municipalities have restrictions on short-term rentals or owner-occupied multi-unit properties. Ensure your house hacking strategy complies with local regulations.

3.3 Consider REITs: Investing in Real Estate Without Direct Ownership

Real Estate Investment Trusts (REITs) offer a way to participate in the real estate market without directly owning and managing properties.

- **The Concept:** REITs pool investor money to purchase and manage income-producing real estate portfolios, such as office buildings, shopping centers, or apartment complexes. REITs are publicly traded on stock exchanges.

Benefits of REITs:

- **Low Barrier to Entry:** REITs offer a relatively low investment compared to directly purchasing a property. You can invest with smaller amounts of money.
- **Diversification:** REITs allow you to invest in a diversified portfolio of real estate across different sectors and geographical locations.
- **Liquidity:** REITs are traded on stock exchanges, offering greater liquidity than directly owning properties. You can easily buy and sell shares.
- **Professional Management:** REITs are managed by experienced professionals who handle property selection, management, and tenant relations.

Considerations for REIT Investors:

- **Market Volatility:** REIT share prices can fluctuate along with the stock market, impacting your investment value.

- **Dividend Dependence:** Your return on investment primarily comes from dividend payouts. Appreciation in share price may be limited compared to direct property ownership.
- **Fees:** REITs typically charge management fees that reduce your overall returns.

3.4 Crowdfunding: A Modern Approach to Real Estate Investment

Real estate crowdfunding platforms offer a novel way for novice investors to participate in the market. Here's how it works:

- **The Process:** Crowdfunding platforms connect investors with real estate developers or sponsors seeking capital for specific projects. Investors pool their funds to finance the project in exchange for potential equity ownership or debt-based returns.

Benefits of Crowdfunding:

- **Low Investment Minimums:** Crowdfunding platforms often have lower investment minimums compared to traditional real estate investments, making it accessible to beginners with limited capital.
- **Diversification:** Some platforms allow you to invest in a variety of projects across different sectors and locations, offering diversification benefits.
- **Passive Investment:** Similar to REITs, you're not directly involved in property management. The project sponsor handles the day-to-day operations.

Considerations for Crowdfunding Investors:

- **Higher Risk:** Crowdfunding investments are generally illiquid and involve a higher degree of risk compared to established asset classes like REITs.
- **Due Diligence is Crucial:** Thoroughly research the platform, the sponsor's track record, and the specific

project details before investing.

- **Limited Regulation:** Crowdfunding regulations may be less stringent compared to traditional investments. Be cautious and invest wisely.

Choosing the Right Strategy for You:

The ideal investment strategy for you depends on your individual circumstances, goals, and risk tolerance. Consider the following factors when making your decision:

- **Available Capital:** How much money can you comfortably invest upfront?
- **Risk Tolerance:** Are you comfortable with the potential for market fluctuations and potential property value declines?
- **Time Commitment:** How much time are you willing to dedicate to property management or researching investment opportunities?
- **Investment Goals:** Are you prioritizing steady cash flow, capital appreciation, or a combination of both?

By understanding your priorities and exploring the diverse investment options available, you can take your first steps towards building a successful real estate portfolio. Remember, starting small, educating yourself, and seeking professional guidance when needed can significantly improve your chances of success in the exciting world of real estate investing.

CHAPTER 4

Mastering the Buy-and-Hold Strategy

Congratulations! You've chosen the buy-and-hold strategy as your foundation for real estate investment..

4.1 Tenant Selection: Finding Reliable Occupants for Your Property

Selecting the right tenants is crucial for maximizing your rental income and minimizing headaches. Here are key strategies for tenant selection:

- **Thorough Screening Process:** Implement a comprehensive screening process that includes credit checks, employment verification, rental history references, and potentially background checks.
- **Clear Lease Agreements:** Clearly outline tenant responsibilities, rent amount and due dates, late

payment fees, maintenance procedures, and lease termination clauses in a well-drafted lease agreement.

- **Security Deposits:** Require a security deposit to cover potential damages beyond normal wear and tear.
- **Effective Advertising:** Utilize online platforms, local listings, and potentially "For Rent" signs to attract qualified tenants.
- **Conducting Interviews:** Take the time to interview prospective tenants to assess their character, financial stability, and overall compatibility with your property.

Additional Tips:

- **Offer Competitive Rents:** Research average rental rates in your area to strike a balance between attracting good tenants and maximizing your return.
- **Consider Offering Incentives:** For well-qualified tenants, offering a signing bonus or slightly lower

rent in exchange for a longer lease term can be beneficial.

- **Maintain a Professional Demeanor:** Present yourself professionally during interactions with potential tenants, fostering a positive relationship from the outset.

By implementing a thorough tenant selection process, you can significantly reduce the risk of encountering problematic tenants who disrupt your cash flow or damage your property.

4.2 Property Management: Delegation or DIY?

The decision to manage your property yourself or hire a professional property management company deserves careful consideration. Here's a breakdown of both approaches:

Do-It-Yourself Property Management:

- **Pros:** Saves on property management fees, allowing

you to keep a larger portion of your rental income.

- **Cons:** Requires significant time commitment for tasks like tenant screening, rent collection, maintenance coordination, repairs, and potentially evictions.
- **Suited For:** Investors with experience in property management, readily available time, and those comfortable handling tenant issues directly.

Hiring a Property Management Company:

- **Pros:** Frees up your time, allowing you to focus on other aspects of your investment portfolio. Experienced property managers can handle tenant relations, maintenance coordination, and ensure legal compliance.
- **Cons:** Property management fees typically range from 8% to 12% of the monthly rent, reducing your overall return on investment.
- **Suited For:** Investors with geographically distant properties, busy schedules, or those who prefer a

hands-off approach to property management.

Factors to Consider When Making Your Decision:

- **Your Time Availability:** Can you realistically dedicate the time needed for effective property management?
- **Your Skillset:** Do you possess the necessary skills and knowledge to handle tenant issues, maintenance coordination, and legal compliance?
- **Property Location:** Is the property geographically convenient for you to manage directly?
- **Property Size and Complexity:** Managing a large multi-unit building may be more suited for a professional property management company.

Finding a Qualified Property Management Company:

- **Seek Referrals:** Ask other real estate investors, your realtor, or mortgage lender for recommendations.
- **Research and Interview Companies:** Research online reviews, compare service offerings and fees,

and conduct interviews to assess their experience and communication style.

- **Check References:** Contact references provided by the property management company to verify their service quality.

By carefully evaluating your needs and preferences, you can determine whether managing your property yourself or hiring a professional is the most suitable approach for your long-term success.

4.3 Maintenance and Repairs: Budgeting and Upkeep Strategies

Proper maintenance is essential for preserving the value of your investment property. Here's how to approach budgeting and repairs:

- **Preventative Maintenance:** Schedule regular inspections and preventative maintenance to identify and address minor issues before they escalate into costly repairs.

- **Budget for Repairs:** Set aside a portion of your rental income each month for anticipated maintenance and repairs. Unexpected expenses can disrupt your cash flow if you're not prepared.

- **Develop a Network of Qualified Contractors:** Build relationships with reliable and experienced plumbers, electricians, and general contractors to ensure timely and cost-effective repairs when needed.

- **DIY Repairs (if applicable):** For minor repairs you're comfortable handling yourself, such as painting or basic plumbing fixes, you can potentially save money on labor costs. However, prioritize safety and avoid tackling repairs beyond your skillset.

- **Emergency Fund:** Maintain a separate emergency fund specifically for unexpected repairs beyond your regular maintenance budget. This helps you avoid scrambling financially in case of a major appliance failure or unforeseen maintenance issue.

Additional Tips:

- **Document Everything:** Keep detailed records of all maintenance work performed, repair invoices, and receipts for materials purchased. This documentation is valuable for tax purposes and future reference.
- **Tenant Responsibilities:** Clearly outline tenant responsibilities for minor maintenance tasks (e.g., changing air filters, garbage disposal usage) within your lease agreement.

By implementing a proactive approach to maintenance and repairs, you can extend the lifespan of your property, minimize costly surprises, and ensure it remains attractive to potential tenants.

4.4 Tax Advantages: Leveraging Tax Benefits of Real Estate Ownership

Real estate ownership offers a multitude of tax benefits that can significantly reduce your taxable income and improve your overall return on investment. Here are some key advantages to understand:

- **Depreciation:** Over time, the IRS allows you to deduct a portion of the property's value from your taxable income each year. This depreciation deduction reduces your tax burden even though the property's overall value may be appreciating.
- **Mortgage Interest Deduction:** The interest you pay on your mortgage can be deducted from your taxable income, further lowering your tax liability.
- **Property Taxes and Operating Expenses:** Property taxes, insurance costs, and certain operating expenses associated with your rental property can also be deducted from your taxable income.

Understanding Tax Implications:

- **Consult a Tax Professional:** Tax laws can be complex, and regulations can change. Consulting with a qualified tax professional is crucial to ensure you're maximizing all available deductions and complying with tax regulations.

- **Record-Keeping is Key:** Maintain meticulous records of all your property-related expenses, including mortgage payments, interest payments, property taxes, repair costs, and depreciation calculations. These records are essential for claiming your deductions when filing your tax return.

By leveraging the tax benefits associated with real estate ownership, you can significantly increase your after-tax returns and enhance the overall profitability of your buy-and-hold investment strategy.

Beyond the Basics:

This chapter has covered the fundamental aspects of mastering the buy-and-hold strategy. As you gain experience and your portfolio grows, you can explore more advanced strategies such as property value optimization through renovations, utilizing 1031 exchanges for tax-deferred property swaps, and potentially hiring property management teams to manage a larger portfolio of properties.

Remember, successful real estate investing is a journey of continuous learning, adaptation, and strategic decision-making. By diligently managing your properties, staying informed about tax regulations, and continuously seeking knowledge, you can unlock the full potential of the buy-and-hold strategy and achieve your long-term wealth creation goals in the exciting world of real estate.

CHAPTER 5

Rehabilitation and Resale: The Fix-and-Flip Approach

The buy-and-hold strategy isn't the only path to success in real estate. This chapter dives into the exciting world of fix-and-flip investing, where you transform undervalued properties into profitable flips. Buckle up, as we explore the key elements of identifying potential fixer-uppers, planning renovations, and ultimately maximizing your return on investment through a successful sale.

5.1 Identifying Fixer-Upper Opportunities: Spotting Diamonds in the Rough

The foundation of a successful fix-and-flip project starts with finding the right property. Here's what you need to consider:

- **Market Analysis:** Research neighborhoods with

strong potential for renovation and resale. Look for areas experiencing revitalization or with rising property values.

- **Identifying Distressed Properties:** Target properties with cosmetic issues, outdated features, or deferred maintenance. Foreclosure listings, expired listings, and probate sales can be good starting points for your search.

- **Considering Property "Bones":** While cosmetic issues are fixable, underlying structural problems like foundation damage or faulty electrical systems can be expensive and time-consuming to address. Prioritize properties with a solid foundation that can be enhanced through renovations.

- **Analyzing Purchase Price:** Factor in the potential renovation costs when making an offer on a fixer-upper. The purchase price plus renovation budget should leave you with a good profit margin after the sale.

Additional Tips:

- **Assemble Your Team:** Build a network of reliable contractors, inspectors, and real estate agents experienced in fix-and-flip projects. Their expertise will be invaluable during the renovation and selling process.

- **Attend Local Auctions and Estate Sales:** Distressed properties can sometimes be found at auctions or estate sales, potentially offering opportunities for below-market entry points. However, proceed with caution and do your due diligence before placing any bids.

By developing a keen eye for identifying undervalued properties with good "bones," you'll be well on your way to sourcing profitable fix-and-flip projects.

5.2 Renovation Planning and Budgeting: Prioritizing Projects and Costs

Once you've secured your fixer-upper, meticulous planning and budgeting are essential for a successful flip. Here's what you need to consider:

- **Prioritization:** Focus on renovations that will add the most value to the property in relation to their cost. Kitchens, bathrooms, and curb appeal improvements typically offer the highest return on investment.
- **Detailed Project Scope and Timeline:** Create a detailed scope of work outlining each renovation project, materials needed, and estimated timelines. This ensures you stay organized and avoid costly delays.
- **Realistic Budgeting:** Factor in labor costs, material prices, permits, and unexpected expenses when creating your renovation budget. Include a buffer of 10-15% to account for unforeseen circumstances.
- **Obtaining Permits:** Research and secure necessary permits for all planned renovations. Failing to do so

can lead to delays and potential fines.

Additional Tips:

- **Consider Value Engineering:** Seek cost-effective alternatives for materials and finishes without compromising quality. There's a difference between "luxury" and "luxurious-looking" on a budget.
- **Get Multiple Contractor Quotes:** Obtain quotes from several qualified contractors to ensure you're getting competitive pricing for your renovation project. Don't always go with the cheapest option, but prioritize value and experience.

By creating a detailed renovation plan and sticking to your budget, you'll minimize surprises and ensure your project stays on track for a profitable flip.

5.3 The Art of the Flip: Marketing and Selling Your Renovated Property

Once your renovations are complete, it's time to showcase

your transformed property and secure a profitable sale. Here's how to effectively market your fix-and-flip:

- **Professional Photography:** High-quality photos showcasing your renovated space are crucial for attracting potential buyers. Invest in professional photography to present your property in its best light.
- **Targeted Marketing:** Utilize online real estate platforms, local advertising, and open houses to reach your target audience of interested buyers. Consider virtual tours if appropriate for the current market.
- **Competitive Pricing:** Research current market trends and similar properties in your area to set a competitive yet attractive asking price. Your realtor can be a valuable resource in determining the optimal pricing strategy.

Additional Tips:

- **Staging for Success:** Stage your renovated property to create an inviting and move-in-ready atmosphere. Consider furniture rentals or consulting a staging professional to maximize the appeal of your space.

- **Highlight Your Renovations:** Clearly communicate the extent and quality of the renovations you've completed in your marketing materials and during open houses. This will help buyers understand the value proposition of your property.

By implementing effective marketing strategies and showcasing the value you've created, you'll increase your chances of attracting qualified buyers and securing a successful sale of your fix-and-flip project.

5.4 Exiting Strategies: Maximizing Profit When Selling Your Investment

The ultimate goal of a fix-and-flip project is to sell your renovated property for a profit. Here are key strategies to maximize your return on investment:

- **Negotiation Skills:** Be prepared to negotiate with potential buyers to achieve a favorable selling price. Understanding your negotiation leverage and the current market conditions is crucial. Consider your realtor's expertise in navigating the negotiation process.

- **Cash vs. Traditional Financing:** While a cash buyer can close the deal faster, you might attract a wider pool of buyers by accepting traditional financing with mortgages. Weigh the pros and cons of each option based on your specific circumstances and market conditions.

- **Considering Multiple Exit Strategies:** In a fast-paced market, you might explore alternative exit strategies beyond a traditional sale. Wholesaling a property (assigning your purchase contract to another investor) can be an option if the market dictates. However, consult with your realtor and legal counsel to ensure compliance with all regulations.

Additional Tips:

- **Track Your Progress:** Maintain detailed records of all renovation costs, permits, and holding expenses throughout the project. This will help you accurately calculate your profit margin when you sell.
- **Factor in Carrying Costs:** Don't forget to factor in property taxes, insurance, and any mortgage payments you incur while holding the property during the renovation and sales process. These ongoing costs affect your overall profitability.

By effectively implementing these strategies, you can ensure a smooth exit from your fix-and-flip project and maximize your profit potential.

5.5 Beyond the Basics: Advanced Fix-and-Flip Strategies

As you gain experience and success with fix-and-flip projects, you can explore more advanced strategies to enhance your returns. Here are a few examples:

- **House Hacking While You Flip:** Live in the fixer-upper while you renovate it, offsetting holding costs and potentially generating rental income if certain renovations are completed first.

- **Fix-and-Hold Option:** If market conditions change, you might decide to hold onto the renovated property as a rental property instead of selling, generating long-term income. However, careful financial analysis is needed before considering this approach.

- **Specialization in a Niche Market:** Develop expertise in flipping a specific property type (e.g., historic homes, mid-century modern) to potentially command higher profit margins.

Remember, the fix-and-flip strategy requires a strong understanding of the real estate market, construction costs, and renovation timelines. By continuously educating yourself, building a reliable network of professionals, and adapting your approach based on market conditions, you can turn the exciting world of fix-and-flip investing into a successful and profitable endeavor.

CHAPTER 6

Advanced Strategies for Experienced Investors

You've mastered the fundamentals of real estate investment and are ready to explore more sophisticated strategies to expand your portfolio and potentially achieve even greater returns.

6.1 BRRRR Method: Renovation, Rental, Refinance, Repeat

The BRRRR method (Buy, Rehabilitate, Rent, Refinance, Repeat) is a powerful strategy that allows you to leverage your investment and build long-term wealth. Here's how it works:

1. **Buy:** Identify a property with strong potential for rental income but in need of renovations.
2. **Rehabilitate:** Make necessary renovations to

improve the property's value and marketability as a rental unit.

3. **Rent:** Lease the renovated property to qualified tenants, generating consistent rental income.
4. **Refinance:** Once the property value increases due to renovations and successful rentals, refinance your mortgage. This frees up a significant portion of your initial investment capital.
5. **Repeat:** Use the freed-up capital from refinancing to purchase another property and repeat the BRRRR process, expanding your portfolio and building wealth over time.

Benefits of the BRRRR Method:

- **Leverages Equity Growth:** Renovations increase property value, allowing you to access more capital through refinancing.
- **Builds Long-Term Wealth:** The BRRRR method allows you to acquire multiple properties over time, creating a growing stream of passive rental income.

- **Improves Cash Flow:** Refinancing with a higher appraised value after renovations can potentially lead to a lower mortgage payment, increasing your monthly cash flow.

Considerations for BRRRR Investors:

- **Requires Significant Capital Upfront:** This strategy necessitates capital for both the initial purchase and renovations.
- **Renovation Expertise is Crucial:** Understanding renovation costs, timelines, and managing potential issues is essential for success.
- **Market Conditions Matter:** Refinancing relies on property value appreciation. Ensure the market supports renovations and rental income generation.

Additional Tips:

- **Develop a Team of Trusted Professionals:** Assemble a reliable network of contractors, property managers, and lenders to navigate the BRRRR process efficiently.

- **Focus on Value-Add Renovations:** Prioritize renovations that significantly improve the property's value and marketability, maximizing your return on investment.

By implementing the BRRRR method strategically, you can significantly accelerate your wealth creation in the real estate market.

6.2 Real Estate Investment Groups (REIGs): Pooling Resources for Bigger Deals

Real Estate Investment Groups (REIGs) offer a way for investors to collaborate and pool their resources to participate in larger real estate projects that might be outside the reach of individual investors. Here's how they work:

- **Structure and Membership:** REIGs can be structured as partnerships, LLCs, or trusts, with membership open to accredited investors who contribute capital.

- **Investment Focus:** REIGs can target various real estate sectors, such as apartment buildings, office buildings, or even development projects.
- **Decision-Making and Management:** REIGs typically have a defined management structure with designated members responsible for decision-making and property management.

Benefits of Participating in REIGs:

- **Access to Larger Deals:** REIGs allow you to invest in properties that might be out of reach for individual investors due to their size or cost.
- **Diversification:** REIGs often invest in a portfolio of properties, offering diversification benefits and potentially mitigating risk.
- **Professional Management:** REIGs often have experienced management teams overseeing acquisitions, renovations, and property operations.

Considerations for REIG Investors:

- **Minimum Investment Requirements:** REIGs often have minimum investment requirements that can be substantial.
- **Less Control:** Investment decisions and management are typically overseen by the REIG's leadership, potentially limiting individual investor control.
- **Fees and Profit Sharing:** REIGs typically charge management fees and have pre-defined profit-sharing structures among members.

Additional Tips:

- **Conduct Thorough Due Diligence:** Carefully research the REIG's track record, investment strategy, and management team before investing.
- **Understand the Legal Structure:** Ensure you comprehend the legal structure of the REIG and your investment rights as a member.

By participating in a well-structured and managed REIG, you can gain access to larger investment opportunities, benefit from professional management, and potentially achieve significant returns on your investment.

6.3 Private Lending: Becoming the Bank for Real Estate Investors

Beyond traditional real estate ownership, you can explore the world of private lending and act as a lender for other real estate investors. Here's how private lending works:

- **The Lending Role:** You provide capital to other investors, typically for fix-and-flip projects or short-term bridge loans, secured by a mortgage or deed of trust on the financed property.
- **Interest Rates and Returns:** Private loans offer potentially higher interest rates compared to traditional savings accounts or bonds. However, these returns come with inherent risks.
- **Loan-to-Value Ratio (LTV):** The LTV ratio refers

to the loan amount compared to the property's appraised value. Lower LTV ratios (meaning you lend a smaller portion of the property value) offer more security in case of borrower default.

Benefits of Private Lending:

- **Potentially High Returns:** Private lending offers the potential for higher returns on your capital compared to traditional investment options.
- **Passive Income Stream:** Regular interest payments from your loans can provide a steady and passive income stream.
- **Security of a Mortgage:** The financed property serves as collateral, mitigating some risk in case the borrower defaults on the loan.

Considerations for Private Lenders:

- **Higher Risk of Default:** There's a chance borrowers may default on their loans, potentially requiring foreclosure proceedings to recover your investment.

- **Careful Loan Structuring:** Proper loan documentation, including clear terms, exit strategies, and potential default clauses, is crucial for protecting your investment.
- **Understanding the Market:** Conduct thorough research on the local real estate market to assess property values and potential risks associated with loan defaults.

Additional Tips:

- **Focus on Experienced Borrowers:** Prioritize lending to experienced real estate investors with a proven track record and a clear exit strategy for their projects.
- **Consider Working with a Loan Servicer:** A loan servicer can handle loan administration tasks like collecting payments and managing defaults, freeing up your time.

By carefully evaluating potential borrowers, structuring

loans strategically, and understanding the inherent risks, private lending can be a lucrative way to generate passive income and participate in the real estate market without directly owning properties.

6.4 Commercial Real Estate: Higher Risks, Potentially Higher Rewards

Commercial real estate encompasses properties used for business purposes, such as office buildings, retail spaces, warehouses, and industrial facilities. This sector offers distinct opportunities and challenges for experienced investors.

- **Types of Commercial Properties:** The commercial real estate market offers a diverse range of property types, each with its own risk-reward profile.
- **Higher Investment Requirements:** Entering the commercial real estate market often requires a significant upfront investment compared to residential properties.

- **Tenant Leases:** Leases in commercial real estate are typically longer than residential leases, offering potentially stable income streams. However, lease negotiations and tenant management can be complex.

Benefits of Commercial Real Estate Investment:

- **Potentially Higher Returns:** Commercial properties can offer higher rental yields compared to residential properties, depending on the specific property type and market conditions.
- **Diversification:** Investing in commercial real estate can add diversification to your overall investment portfolio, potentially mitigating risk.
- **Long-Term Leases:** Longer lease terms with established businesses can provide predictable and stable income streams.

Considerations for Commercial Real Estate Investors:

- **Market Specificity:** Commercial real estate markets

can be highly localized, requiring in-depth research and understanding of specific property sectors and tenant demographics.

- **Higher Management Complexity:** Managing commercial properties can be more complex than residential properties, potentially requiring specialized property management expertise.
- **Vacancy Risks:** Vacancies in commercial properties can significantly impact your cash flow, so vacancy rates and lease structures are crucial factors to consider.

Additional Tips:

- **Seek Professional Guidance:** Consulting with experienced commercial real estate brokers and property managers can be invaluable for navigating the intricacies of this market sector.
- **Focus on Strong Locations:** Prioritize properties in well-established locations with high occupancy rates and strong tenant demand.

By carefully assessing the risks and rewards, conducting thorough market research, and potentially partnering with experienced professionals, commercial real estate can be a path to achieving significant returns in the world of real estate investing.

This chapter has explored advanced strategies for experienced investors seeking to expand their horizons beyond the fundamentals. Remember, continuous learning, strategic planning, and adapting to market conditions are essential for success in any real estate investment endeavor. As you gain experience and navigate the exciting world of advanced strategies, you can unlock even greater potential for wealth creation and achieve your long-term real estate investment goals.

CHAPTER 7

FINANCING YOUR REAL ESTATE INVESTMENTS

Financing is the lifeblood of real estate investment. This chapter equips you with the knowledge to navigate the various financing options available for acquiring and holding your investment properties. Whether you're a seasoned investor or just starting out, understanding the different loan types and their qualifications is crucial for making informed investment decisions.

7.1 Traditional Mortgage Options: Understanding Loan Types and Qualifications

Traditional mortgages from banks and credit unions are the most common financing option for real estate investment. Here's a breakdown of key loan types and considerations:

- **Conventional Loans:** These are the most common

mortgages, typically requiring a 20% down payment and offering competitive interest rates. Qualifying for a conventional loan requires a good credit score (typically above 670), steady income verification, and a strong debt-to-income ratio (DTI).

- **Federal Housing Administration (FHA) Loans:** FHA loans are government-insured mortgages that allow for a lower down payment (as low as 3.5%) compared to conventional loans. However, they come with additional upfront fees and mortgage insurance premiums.
- **Veterans Administration (VA) Loans:** VA loans are a benefit program for veterans offering zero-down-payment options and competitive interest rates. Eligibility is restricted to qualified veterans and active-duty service members meeting specific service requirements.

Additional Considerations When Choosing a Traditional Mortgage:

- **Fixed-Rate vs. Adjustable-Rate Mortgages (ARMs):** Fixed-rate mortgages offer consistent monthly payments throughout the loan term. ARMs offer lower initial rates but can adjust up or down over time, potentially impacting your monthly payments.

- **Loan-to-Value Ratio (LTV):** The LTV ratio compares your loan amount to the appraised value of the property. Lower LTVs (meaning you borrow a smaller portion of the property value) typically qualify for more favorable loan terms.

- **Private Mortgage Insurance (PMI):** If your down payment on a conventional loan is less than 20%, you'll likely be required to pay PMI, which protects the lender in case of default. Once your equity reaches 20%, PMI is typically removed.

Tips for Qualifying for Traditional Mortgages:

- **Maintain a Good Credit Score:** A strong credit history is essential for securing favorable loan terms.

Aim for a credit score above 670 for conventional loans and consult a credit counselor if needed to improve your score.

- **Demonstrate Stable Income:** Verifiable income through employment or self-employment documentation is crucial. Lenders will analyze your income to ensure you can comfortably afford the monthly mortgage payments.

- **Manage Your Debt-to-Income Ratio (DTI):** Your DTI ratio compares your total monthly debt payments (including housing expenses) to your gross monthly income. Aim for a DTI below 36% to increase your chances of qualifying for a loan.

By understanding the different traditional mortgage options, their qualifications, and the factors influencing loan terms, you can make informed decisions when financing your real estate investments.

7.2 Hard Money Lenders: Alternative Financing for

Quick Deals

Hard money lenders are private lenders who offer short-term, high-interest rate loans for real estate investments. They can be a valuable tool for situations where traditional financing might not be suitable.

- **Use Cases for Hard Money Lenders:** Hard money loans are often used for fix-and-flip projects due to their quick turnaround times and flexible qualification requirements. They can also be used for investment purchases requiring fast action due to competitive market conditions.
- **Higher Interest Rates and Fees:** Be prepared for significantly higher interest rates and upfront fees compared to traditional mortgages. Hard money loans are intended to be short-term solutions, and the high costs should be factored into your investment strategy.
- **Focus on Project Potential:** Hard money lenders primarily focus on the property's potential value

after renovation or resale rather than your credit score or income. A solid renovation plan and a clear exit strategy are crucial for securing a hard money loan.

Important Note: Hard money lending is a specialized field. Conduct thorough research, compare rates and terms from multiple lenders, and ensure you have a clear understanding of the loan terms and repayment structure before entering into a hard money loan agreement.

7.3 House Hacking Mortgages: Financing Strategies for Owner-Occupied Investments

House hacking involves living in a multi-unit property while renting out the remaining units to generate rental income that helps offset your mortgage payment. Here, specific mortgage options can be beneficial:

- **FHA Multi-Unit Mortgages:** FHA loans allow for financing multi-unit properties (up to four units) with a lower down payment (as low as 3.5%). The rental income from the additional units can be factored into your qualifying income when applying for the loan.

- **Conventional Investment Property Mortgages:** These mortgages are specifically designed for investment properties and typically require a higher down payment (around 15-20%) compared to owner-occupied loans. However, they may offer competitive interest rates.

Qualifying for House Hacking Mortgages:

The qualifying process for house hacking mortgages is similar to traditional mortgages, but with additional considerations:

- **Occupancy Requirements:** FHA multi-unit mortgages require you to live in one of the units as your primary residence.
- **Rental Income Projections:** When applying for the

loan, you'll need to provide realistic projections of rental income from the non-owner-occupied units. This income will be factored into your debt-to-income ratio (DTI) to determine your eligibility.

- **Property Appraisal:** The property will be appraised considering both the value of the entire property and the potential rental income from the non-occupied units.

Additional Tips for House Hacking Mortgages:

- **Consider Future Conversion:** If you plan to eventually convert the property to a fully rented investment property, choose a mortgage that allows for such a transition without refinancing.
- **Factor in Maintenance Costs:** Remember to factor in additional maintenance and utility costs associated with a multi-unit property when calculating your overall investment viability.

By understanding the specific financing options available for house hacking and carefully considering the qualification requirements, you can leverage this strategy to enter the real estate market while minimizing your upfront financial burden.

7.4 Creative Financing Techniques: Seller Financing and Lease Options

Beyond traditional and hard money lenders, there are creative financing techniques that can be explored for real estate investment deals. Here are two examples:

- **Seller Financing:** In seller financing, the seller acts as the bank and finances a portion of the purchase price for the buyer. This can be an option if the seller is motivated to sell quickly or if traditional financing is unavailable.
- **Lease Options:** A lease option gives you the right, but not the obligation, to purchase a property at a predetermined price within a specific timeframe. In

exchange for this option, you typically pay the seller a non-refundable fee and potentially a monthly rent. This can be a way to control a property while securing additional time to arrange traditional financing.

Important Considerations for Creative Financing:

- **Carefully Review Agreements:** Creative financing arrangements often involve complex contracts. Consult with a lawyer experienced in real estate transactions to ensure you understand the terms and implications before entering into such agreements.

- **Potential for Higher Costs:** Seller financing may come with higher interest rates compared to traditional mortgages. Lease options involve upfront fees and potentially lost rent payments if you decide not to exercise the purchase option.

- **Alignment of Interests:** Ensure your interests align with the seller in a seller-financing arrangement. Clearly defined communication and realistic expectations are crucial for a successful outcome.

Final Thoughts on Financing:

Financing is a critical aspect of real estate investment. By understanding the different options available, from traditional mortgages to creative financing techniques, you can equip yourself to make informed decisions and secure the funding necessary to build your real estate portfolio. Remember, carefully evaluate the pros and cons of each financing option, considering factors like interest rates, fees, qualification requirements, and your overall investment strategy. As you gain experience and navigate the dynamic world of real estate financing, you'll be well-positioned to identify and leverage the most suitable financing solutions to fuel your investment journey.

CHAPTER 8

Legal Considerations and Asset Protection

Real estate investment, while potentially lucrative, involves navigating a legal landscape.

8.1 Entity Formation: Choosing the Right Structure for Your Investments

The legal structure you choose for holding your real estate investments can significantly impact your taxes, liability protection, and management flexibility. Here's a breakdown of common entity types:

- **Sole Proprietorship:** The simplest structure, but offers no personal liability protection. All business debts and liabilities fall on the owner. Not recommended for real estate investment due to the high-risk nature.

- **Limited Liability Company (LLC):** A popular choice offering personal liability protection for the owner(s). LLCs are relatively easy to form and manage, with flexible profit and loss (P&L) pass-through taxation.

- **S Corporation (S-Corp):** A more complex structure that can be beneficial for tax purposes under certain conditions. S-Corps separate business income from the owner's personal income, potentially leading to tax advantages. However, they come with stricter regulations and filing requirements.

Factors to Consider When Choosing an Entity:

- **Liability Protection:** LLCs offer strong personal liability protection, shielding your personal assets from business debts.

- **Tax Implications:** Consult a tax professional to understand the tax implications of each entity type. Tax considerations will vary depending on your individual circumstances and investment goals.

- **Management Flexibility:** LLCs offer more management flexibility compared to S-Corps, which have stricter ownership and management structure requirements.

Additional Tips:

- **Consult with a Legal Professional:** Seek guidance from an attorney experienced in real estate law to determine the most suitable entity structure for your specific investment needs.
- **Consider Future Growth:** If you plan on expanding your investment portfolio, choose an entity structure that can accommodate future growth without requiring complex restructuring.

By carefully considering the factors mentioned above and consulting with a legal professional, you can select the right entity type to optimize asset protection, tax benefits, and management flexibility for your real estate investments.

8.2 Landlord-Tenant Laws: Understanding Your Rights and Responsibilities

As a landlord, you have specific rights and responsibilities outlined by local and state landlord-tenant laws. Understanding these laws is crucial for managing your rental properties effectively and avoiding legal disputes.

- **Key Areas of Landlord-Tenant Law:** These laws typically cover aspects like tenant screening, lease agreements, security deposits, habitability standards, eviction procedures, and rent collection rights.
- **Staying Up-to-Date:** Landlord-tenant laws can change over time. Stay informed by researching local and state regulations or consulting with a property management professional.
- **Tenant Screening:** A thorough tenant screening process helps mitigate risks associated with non-payment of rent or property damage. Background checks, credit checks, and verifying references are common practices.

Additional Tips:

- **Clear and Comprehensive Lease Agreements:** Utilize well-drafted lease agreements that clearly outline tenant responsibilities, rent payment terms, maintenance procedures, and expectations for both parties.

- **Proper Security Deposit Handling:** Adhere to local regulations regarding security deposits, including collection, deductions for damages (if applicable), and timely return of the deposit upon lease termination.

- **Maintain Habitable Properties:** As a landlord, you have a legal obligation to provide tenants with habitable living conditions. This includes functioning utilities, proper sanitation, and addressing safety hazards.

By familiarizing yourself with landlord-tenant laws, implementing proper tenant screening procedures, and maintaining your properties, you can minimize legal issues and foster positive relationships with your tenants.

8.3 Real Estate Contracts: Navigating the Legal Landscape with Confidence

Real estate transactions involve various legal contracts, from purchase agreements to repair contracts. Understanding these contracts and their implications is essential for protecting your interests.

- **Common Real Estate Contracts:** These include purchase agreements, seller disclosure forms, inspection reports, repair agreements, and lease agreements (for rentals).
- **Key Contractual Elements:** Pay close attention to details like purchase price, closing costs, contingencies (clauses outlining conditions that must be met before the sale is finalized), repair responsibilities, and termination clauses.
- **Importance of Legal Review:** Never sign a real estate contract without a thorough review by a

qualified real estate attorney. They can explain the legal implications of each clause and negotiate terms in your best interest.

Additional Tips:

- **Don't Be Afraid to Ask Questions:** If there's anything unclear in a contract, don't hesitate to ask your realtor or attorney for clarification. Ensure you fully understand your rights and obligations before signing.
- **Keep Copies of All Documents:** Maintain a well-organized file of all signed contracts, inspection reports, and other relevant documents related to your real estate investments. These can be crucial for future reference or potential legal proceedings.

By prioritizing legal review, understanding key contractual elements, and maintaining clear documentation, you can navigate the world of real estate contracts with confidence and minimize the risk of encountering unforeseen issues.

8.4 Insurance Strategies: Protecting Your Investments from Unexpected Events

Real estate investment involves inherent risks. A comprehensive insurance strategy can safeguard your assets and provide financial security in the event of unexpected occurrences.

- **Essential Insurance Coverage:**

    - **Property Insurance:** Protects your property from damage caused by fire, theft, vandalism, and other covered perils. Consider both dwelling coverage for the structure itself and liability coverage to protect against injuries sustained by others on your property.
    - **Landlord Insurance:** Provides additional coverage specific to rental properties, including protection against lost rental income due to vacancy or tenant damage beyond normal wear and tear.

- **Errors and Omissions (E&O) Insurance:** Protects you from lawsuits alleging negligence in your role as a landlord. This can be particularly relevant if you manage your own rental properties.

- **Additional Considerations:**

  - **Flood Insurance:** Flood insurance may be required in certain areas or for properties located in flood plains.
  - **Umbrella Insurance:** An umbrella policy can provide additional liability coverage beyond the limits of your standard property or landlord insurance.
  - **Review and Adjust Coverage Regularly:** As your portfolio grows or property values change, revisit your insurance coverage limits and types to ensure adequate protection.

Additional Tips:

- **Shop Around and Compare Rates:** Obtain quotes from multiple insurance providers to find the most competitive rates for the coverage you need.
- **Work with a Reputable Insurance Agent:** An experienced insurance agent can help you tailor an insurance plan that effectively addresses your specific investment property risks.
- **Maintain Good Records:** Documenting maintenance records and repairs can be beneficial in the event of an insurance claim.

By implementing a comprehensive insurance strategy and working with qualified insurance professionals, you can achieve peace of mind knowing your real estate investments are protected against potential financial losses due to unforeseen events.

navigating the legal and asset protection aspects of real

estate investment requires knowledge, preparation, and proactiveness. By understanding entity structures, landlord-tenant laws, the importance of legal review in contracts, and implementing a comprehensive insurance strategy, you can safeguard your assets, minimize legal risks, and make informed decisions throughout your real estate investment journey. Remember, consulting with qualified legal and financial professionals throughout the process is paramount for achieving success in the exciting world of real estate.

CHAPTER 9

Weathering the Storm: Managing Risk in Real Estate

Real estate, while a potentially rewarding investment path, is not without its challenges.

9.1 Market Fluctuations: Strategies for Volatile Economic Conditions

Real estate markets are cyclical, experiencing periods of growth followed by inevitable downturns. Here's how to prepare for and navigate market fluctuations:

- **Understanding Market Cycles:** Educate yourself on historical market trends and economic indicators to anticipate potential shifts. This knowledge can help you make informed investment decisions and adjust your strategy accordingly.

- **Diversification is Key:** Don't concentrate your

investments in a single geographic location or property type. Spread your portfolio across different markets and property types to mitigate risk if one sector experiences a downturn.

- **Focus on Long-Term Strategy:** Real estate is a long-term investment. While short-term fluctuations can be concerning, maintain a long-term perspective and avoid panic selling during market downturns. High-quality properties in desirable locations tend to weather economic storms better.

Additional Tips:

- **Build Cash Reserves:** Having a healthy cash reserve allows you to weather temporary periods of vacancy or lower rental income during economic downturns. Aim to save enough to cover several months of mortgage payments and potential unexpected expenses.
- **Stay Informed:** Continuously monitor market trends, economic news, and interest rate changes to

stay updated and adapt your strategy as needed. Utilize resources like industry reports, attend real estate investment seminars, and network with experienced investors.

By understanding market cycles, diversifying your portfolio, and maintaining a long-term perspective, you can navigate market fluctuations and position yourself for success even in challenging economic conditions.

9.2 Vacancy Rates and Tenant Turnover: Minimizing Rental Income Disruptions

Vacancies and tenant turnover can significantly disrupt your rental income stream. Here are strategies to minimize these disruptions:

- **Competitive Rents and Attractive Properties:** Conduct thorough market research to determine fair and competitive rental rates for your properties. Invest in maintaining the curb appeal and functionality of your rentals to attract and retain high-quality tenants.

- **Thorough Tenant Screening:** Implement a rigorous tenant screening process, including credit checks, background checks, and verifying references. This helps mitigate the risk of encountering problematic tenants who might damage your property or pay rent late.

- **Offer Competitive Lease Agreements:** Consider offering competitive lease terms, such as multi-year leases with incremental rent increases, to incentivize tenants to stay longer and reduce turnover.

Additional Tips:

- **Maintain Open Communication with Tenants:** Build positive relationships with your tenants by being responsive to their needs and addressing maintenance issues promptly. Satisfied tenants are more likely to renew their leases and less likely to cause damage to the property.

- **Consider Professional Property Management:** For a larger portfolio or if you lack the time for day-to-day management, consider hiring a reputable property management company. They can handle tenant screening, rent collection, maintenance requests, and other tasks, freeing up your time and potentially reducing vacancy rates.

By implementing these strategies, you can minimize vacancy periods, retain tenants for longer terms, and achieve a more predictable and stable rental income stream from your investment properties.

9.3 Property Damage and Maintenance Issues: Building Reserves and Risk Mitigation

Unexpected property damage and maintenance issues are inevitable realities of real estate ownership. Here's how to prepare for these situations:

- **Budget for Maintenance and Repairs:** Factor in

regular maintenance costs and potential repairs into your overall investment budget. Setting aside funds proactively helps you address issues as they arise without straining your cash flow.

- **Building Capital Reserves:** Consider establishing a capital reserve fund specifically for major repairs or unexpected events like roof replacements or appliance breakdowns. This financial buffer prevents you from scrambling for funds when significant repairs become necessary.

- **Regular Inspections and Preventative Maintenance:** Conduct regular property inspections to identify and address minor issues before they escalate into larger, more expensive problems. Preventative maintenance can significantly reduce the risk of major repairs and extend the lifespan of your property's components.

Additional Tips:

- **Screen Contractors Carefully:** When hiring

contractors for repairs, obtain multiple quotes, check references, and ensure they are licensed and insured.

- **Maintain Detailed Records:** Keep meticulous records of all maintenance work performed, repairs completed, and associated costs. This documentation can be beneficial for tax purposes and future reference.

By budgeting for maintenance, building reserves, and prioritizing preventative maintenance, you can mitigate the financial impact of property damage and repairs, protecting your investment and avoiding unnecessary stress.

9.4 Legal Challenges: Addressing Lawsuits and Disputes

Despite best efforts, legal challenges or disputes with tenants, contractors, or even neighbors can arise in real estate investment. Here's how to approach such situations:

- **Proactive Risk Mitigation:** The best defense

against legal challenges is to be proactive. Following best practices in tenant screening, clear lease agreements, proper maintenance, and adhering to fair housing laws can significantly reduce the risk of disputes.

- **Importance of Documentation:** Maintain clear and detailed documentation of all lease agreements, maintenance records, communication with tenants, and any relevant financial records. This documentation can be crucial evidence in the event of a legal dispute.

- **Seek Legal Counsel Promptly:** If a legal challenge arises, don't hesitate to consult with an attorney experienced in real estate law. Early legal guidance can help you navigate the situation effectively and protect your rights.

Additional Tips:

- **Consider Landlord Insurance:** Landlord insurance can provide some protection against legal costs associated with lawsuits from tenants, such as slip-and-fall injuries or accusations of discrimination.

- **Focus on Dispute Resolution:** Whenever possible, attempt to resolve disputes with tenants or other parties amicably through open communication and negotiation. This can be more cost-effective and time-saving than protracted legal battles.

By prioritizing risk mitigation strategies, maintaining thorough documentation, and seeking legal counsel when necessary, you can minimize the disruption and financial impact of potential legal challenges that may arise during your real estate investment journey.

The real estate market offers significant potential rewards, but like any investment, it comes with inherent risks. By understanding the potential challenges, implementing risk management strategies, and proactively preparing for unforeseen circumstances, you can navigate the ups and downs of the market, minimize disruptions to your income flow, and protect your assets. Remember, continuous learning, strategic planning, and adaptation are key to navigating the ever-changing landscape of real estate investment. With a well-defined plan, a risk-mitigation mindset, and the willingness to seek professional guidance when needed, you can weather any storm and achieve long-term success in the exciting world of real estate.

CHAPTER 10

The Long Game: Building a Sustainable Real Estate Portfolio

Real estate investment is a marathon, not a sprint..

10.1 Diversification Strategies: Spreading Your Investments Across Markets and Property Types

Don't put all your eggs in one basket! Diversification is a cornerstone of successful real estate investment. Here's why and how to diversify your portfolio:

- **Mitigating Market Risks:** Real estate markets are geographically localized, and economic conditions can vary significantly across regions. Spreading your investments across different markets reduces your reliance on the performance of any single location.
- **Hedging Against Property Type Fluctuations:** The

performance of different property types can fluctuate over time. Diversifying across property types, such as residential rentals, commercial spaces, or industrial facilities, offers protection against downturns in any specific sector.

- **Investment Strategies and Risk Tolerance:** Consider your investment goals and risk tolerance when choosing property types. For example, single-family homes may offer lower risk and steady rental income, while apartment buildings can provide higher potential returns but also come with increased management complexity.

Diversification Strategies:

- **Geographic Diversity:** Invest in properties located in different cities or even states to mitigate the impact of localized economic downturns.
- **Property Type Diversification:** Consider a mix of residential (single-family homes, multi-unit buildings), commercial (office spaces, retail stores),

or industrial properties to diversify your income streams and risk profile.

- **Investment Options:** Explore diversification beyond direct property ownership. Consider Real Estate Investment Trusts (REITs) that pool investor funds to acquire and manage a variety of real estate assets.

Additional Tips:

- **Conduct Market Research:** Carefully research different markets and property types before investing. Analyze factors like vacancy rates, rental income potential, and long-term growth prospects.
- **Start Small and Scale Up:** Begin with a manageable portfolio and gradually add properties or explore different investment options as you gain experience and confidence.

By implementing a well-diversified portfolio strategy, you can mitigate risk, balance your investment goals with risk tolerance, and position yourself for long-term success in the ever-evolving real estate market.

10.2 Goal Setting and Portfolio Rebalancing: Keeping Your Investments Aligned with Objectives

Successful real estate investment requires clear goals and ongoing portfolio management. Here's how to stay on track:

- **Defining Your Investment Goals:** Are you aiming for steady cash flow through rental income, long-term capital appreciation, or a combination of both? Clearly defined goals will guide your investment decisions.
- **Developing a Long-Term Investment Plan:** Create a roadmap for your portfolio growth, considering factors like your investment horizon, risk tolerance, and desired level of involvement in property management.
- **Periodic Portfolio Rebalancing:** Over time, the

performance of different assets within your portfolio might change. Periodic rebalancing involves selling off assets that have outperformed expectations and reinvesting the proceeds in underperforming areas to maintain your desired risk profile and asset allocation.

Additional Tips:

- **Track Your Portfolio Performance:** Monitor the performance of your investments regularly. Utilize spreadsheets or portfolio management software to track key metrics like rental income, property values, and overall portfolio performance.
- **Stay Informed About Market Trends:** Continuously educate yourself about evolving market conditions, emerging investment opportunities, and relevant legal or tax changes that might impact your portfolio.

By setting clear goals, developing a long-term plan, and

practicing regular portfolio rebalancing, you can ensure your investments remain aligned with your objectives and contribute to achieving your financial aspirations over time.

10.3 Building a Team of Experts: Realtors, Property Managers, and Financial Advisors

Building a successful real estate portfolio often involves leveraging the expertise of qualified professionals. Here's how the right team can benefit you:

- **Realtors:** Experienced realtors provide valuable assistance in property search, negotiation, and closing transactions. They can help you identify properties that meet your investment criteria and secure them at competitive prices.
- **Property Managers:** Property managers can handle the day-to-day operations of your rental properties, including tenant screening, rent collection, maintenance coordination, and ensuring compliance

with local regulations. This frees up your time and allows you to focus on growing your portfolio.

- **Financial Advisors:** Financial advisors can offer valuable insights on tax implications of real estate investments, help you develop a comprehensive financial plan, and ensure your real estate strategy aligns with your overall financial goals.

Finding the Right Professionals:

- **Seek Referrals:** Ask friends, family, or other investors for recommendations on qualified realtors, property managers, and financial advisors.

- **Conduct Interviews:** Schedule interviews with potential team members to assess their experience, qualifications, and approach to real estate investment. Ensure they align with your investment goals and communication style.

Additional Tips:

- **Clearly Define Roles and Expectations:** Establish

clear communication channels and expectations with each team member. Outline their specific responsibilities and how they will report to you.

- **Maintain Open Communication:** Regularly communicate with your team, provide updates on your investment goals, and don't hesitate to ask questions or seek their guidance as needed.

By assembling a team of qualified professionals, you can leverage their expertise, gain valuable insights, and free up your time to focus on strategic decision-making and growing your real estate portfolio.

10.4 The Future of Real Estate: Emerging Trends and Technological Advancements

The real estate industry is constantly evolving, with new technologies and trends shaping the investment landscape. Here's a glimpse into the future:

- **PropTech (Property Technology):** Emerging

technologies like virtual tours, online rental applications, and smart home features are transforming how properties are marketed, managed, and occupied.

- **Real Estate Crowdfunding:** Crowdfunding platforms allow individuals to pool smaller investment amounts to participate in larger real estate projects, potentially democratizing access to this asset class.

- **Data Analytics and AI:** Real estate investors are increasingly leveraging data analytics and artificial intelligence to identify undervalued markets, predict future trends, and optimize property management strategies.

Staying Ahead of the Curve:

- **Embrace Continuous Learning:** Stay informed about emerging trends and technological advancements in the real estate industry. Attend industry conferences, read relevant publications, and network with experienced investors to stay ahead of the curve.

- **Consider How These Trends Affect Your Strategy:** Evaluate how these trends might impact your investment approach. For example, PropTech might allow you to manage geographically distant properties more effectively, while crowdfunding platforms could open doors to new investment opportunities.

By understanding and adapting to the evolving real estate landscape, you can position yourself to capitalize on emerging trends and technological advancements to achieve long-term success in your real estate investment journey.

Conclusion

Building a sustainable real estate portfolio requires a long-term perspective, a commitment to continuous learning, and the ability to adapt to changing market conditions. By implementing the strategies outlined in this chapter, you can navigate the complexities of real estate investment, build a well-diversified portfolio, and achieve your financial goals. Remember, the key to success lies in setting clear objectives, building a team of experts, staying informed about market trends, and making informed decisions that contribute to your long-term vision. With dedication, perseverance, and a strategic approach, you can transform real estate investment into a powerful tool for building wealth and achieving financial security for your future.

ABOUT THE AUTHOR

Riley Anderson is a multifaceted individual, blending the roles of business guru, writer, and motivational speaker. With a keen insight into the intricacies of publishing and a talent for inspiring others, Riley has become a sought-after figure in both the literary and entrepreneurial worlds.

In terms of education, Riley holds a degree in Business Administration with a focus on Marketing from a reputable university. This educational background, coupled with years of practical experience, has equipped Riley with the knowledge and skills needed to navigate the competitive landscape of both the business and publishing industries. Whether through written works or captivating speeches, Riley's aim is to empower and guide individuals on their journey to success

www.ingramcontent.com/pod-product-compliance
Lightning Source LLC
Chambersburg PA
CBHW050109230526
45470CB00004B/1748